our Planet Earth

CONSERVATION AND NATURAL RESOURCES

Please visit our web site at: www.garethstevens.com
For a free color catalog describing Gareth Stevens Publishing's list of high-quality books , call 1-800-542-2595 (USA) or 1-800-387-3178 (Canada). Gareth Stevens Publishing's fax: 1-877-542-2596.

Library of Congress Cataloging-in-Publication Data

Conserve
    Conservation and natural resources.
        p. cm. — (Discovery Channel school science: our planet Earth)
    Originally published: Conserve. Bethesda, Md.: Discovery Enterprises. © 2000.
    Summary: Discusses some of the Earth's natural resources, threats to their existence, and efforts to protect them. Includes related activities.
    ISBN-13: 978-0-8368-3377-5   ISBN-10: 0-8368-3377-5 (lib. bdg.)
    1. Conservation of natural resources—Juvenile literature. [1. Conservation of natural resources.] I. Title. II. Series.
    S940.C66 2004
    333.72—dc22

                                 2003059210

This edition first published in 2004 by
Gareth Stevens Publishing
A Weekly Reader® Company
1 Reader's Digest Road
Pleasantville, NY 10570-7000 USA

This U.S. edition copyright © 2004 by Gareth Stevens, Inc. First published in 2000 as *Conserve: The Natural Resources Files* by Discovery Enterprises, LLC, Bethesda, Maryland. © 2000 by Discovery Communications, Inc.

Further resources for students and educators available at
www.discoveryschool.com

Designed by BILL SMITH STUDIO
Creative Director: Ron Leighton
Designers: Nick Stone, Sonia Gauba, Darren D'Agostino, Dmitri Kushnirsky, Bill Wilson, Joe Bartos
Photo Editors: Jennifer Friel, Scott Haag
Art Buyers: Paula Radding, Marianne Tozzo

Gareth Stevens Editor: Betsy Rasmussen
Gareth Stevens Art Director: Tammy West
Technical Advisor: Emily Watson

Writers: Jackie Ball, Paul Barnett, Justine Ciovacco, David Diefendorf, Ruth Greenstein, Uechi Ng, Anna Prokos, Tom Ranieri, Denise Vega

Editor: Justine Ciovacco.

Photographs: Cover, A & L Sinibaldi/Tony Stone Images; pp. 2, 4, 5, Bronx River, G. Paul Bennet/NYT Picture; p. 3, globe, © MapArt; pp. 3, 8, Aldo Leopold, Aldo Leopold Foundation; pp. 6–7, Redwoods, COREL; p. 8, John Muir stamp, U.S. Post Office; p. 13, dust-bowl, © Bettmann/CORBIS; p. 15, Exxon Valdez (3/89), © Natalie Fobe/CORBIS; pp. 16–17, Rick Dove, Neuse River Foundation, Inc.; p. 18, COREL; p. 19, Hudson River, ©Bettmann/CORBIS; p. 19, Cryptobiotic soil, © Judie Chrobak-Cox; p. 19, Olympic National Park, COREL; pp. 20–21, Amazon Rain Forest, © Wolfgang Bayer/DCI; p. 25, COREL; p. 26, Sen. Gaylord Nelson, Senate Historical Office; p. 26, Earth Day,

© Jay Syverson/CORBIS; p. 30, garbage barge, AP Photo/David Book; p. 30, Edwards Dam, © Associated Press; all other photos: © PhotoDisc.

Illustrators: p. 16, water cycle, Chris Burke; p. 28, Lee MacLeod.

Acknowledgments: p. 8, excerpt from A SAND COUNTY ALMANAC. © 1948 by Aldo Leopold. Reprinted by permission of Oxford University Press; p. 8, excerpt from OUR NATIONAL PARKS. © 1901 by John Muir. Reprinted by permission of Houghton, Mifflin & Co.; p. 8, excerpt from MY FIRST SUMMER IN THE SIERRA, by John Muir. Foreward © 1988 by Frederick Turner. Reprinted with permission of Sierra Club Books; p. 12, DUST STORM DISASTER by Woody Guthrie, © 1960, Ludlow Music. p. 27, "Easy as One , Two, Tree!" information from KID HEROES OF THE ENVIRONMENT. © 1991 by The EarthEorks Groupe. Reprinted by permission of the EarthWorks Press.

Discovery CHANNEL SCHOOL SCIENCE

CONTENTS

CONSERVATION AND NATURAL RESOURCES

The best things in life are free, right? Look outside: You can sit under a tree, take a deep breath of air, dig up the dirt, splash in a puddle—and you don't have to pay a cent. Plus, this stuff has been around practically forever. The same water has been cycling Earth for billions of years. From the same soil on which our ancestors planted crops sprout plants we use for food today. Some of the most majestic trees have been around for thousands of years.

We have a right to enjoy all of these natural resources fully, don't we? Cut lumber is useful for paper, buildings, and cozy fires. Water flows freely with the turn of a faucet. So, what's the problem? All of our "enjoyment" *does* have a cost: Natural resources can't replenish themselves as quickly as we can use them up. And human activities have hurt the supply of some resources.

Discovery Channel's CONSERVATION and NATURAL RESOURCES explains the issues that concern Earth and affect every living—and nonliving— thing. You are about to learn a secret nature lovers know: The land is ripe with treasures . . . and you can affect all of them.

This man knows nature . . .
See page 9.

Final Project

Natural Resources

In November 1999, New York's parks commissioner, Henry J. Stern, joined with other officials from local businesses and neighborhood groups to discuss a major environmental project. The setting was the scene of a "crime": the very polluted Bronx River.

Like too many waterways across the United States, the Bronx River has become a dumping ground for everything from cars and tires to appliances and waste from nearby businesses. It doesn't help that the river is located next to a parkway, filled every day, all day, with cars. But humans and their activities are truly to blame for the "open sewer" that the river has become and the fact that it has been this way for more than one hundred years.

The project the parks commissioner was announcing—to restore the Bronx River—is expected to cost $60 million and take ten years. The result should be plenty of green-leafed trees and bushes, clean water filled with aquatic life, and riverside trailways for bikes. This kind of long-term project is part of what's called environmentalism. That's the movement to conserve natural resources, prevent pollution, and encourage responsible land use. Conservationists are people like the parks commissioner and the local residents who work toward fixing and protecting the land, water, trees, and plants that make up our natural resources. Actually, some of the earliest conservationists were Native Americans. They have always believed nature is a precious gift with a spirit that needs to be protected.

In the early 1900s, U.S. conservationists began establishing national parks and forests. But it wasn't until after World War II that concern for pollution and dwindling energy resources became a public concern. This increased interest in the environment focused on a bigger idea: protecting Earth's self-renewal. In other words, don't just clean the mess we've created . . . don't make a mess in the first place.

Environmental concerns have since inspired important laws, including the National Environmental Protection Act (1970), which created the Environmental Protection Agency to develop nationwide standards for the quality of natural resources. Many private organizations, such as the Sierra Club and National Audubon Society, have helped the process by informing the public and encouraging the passage of laws on environmental causes. And you? Everyday activities, such as recycling and conserving natural resources, help keep Earth healthy. This book will tell you more about the conservation movement, and what you can do to help.

A giant crane pulls a rusted car out of the Bronx River. Chemicals from the car and other items tossed into the river have polluted the water, soil, and trees in the area.

LEGEND OF THE TALL

Q: We're taking a walk through the Redwood Forest in northern California to speak with a redwood, one of the biggest trees in the world. Hello up there!

A: Hey, Shorty. What's up—besides me?

Q: You ARE tall. How tall are you, anyway?

A: I stand—make that, tower majestically—more than 267 feet in the air. That's about 81 meters. Or picture forty-five tall men standing on each other's shoulders. Or, because you'll never see forty-five tall men doing that, how about thinking of that tree they light up in New York City at the holidays? Now multiply its height by five or six.

Q: That's tall, all right. How did you get so big?

A: Now, that's what I call a long story. Literally. I've been around for something like 3000—maybe 4000—years. Hard to say exactly. I stopped counting a while ago.

Anyway, I owe a lot of my long life to what I'm wrapped up in: my bark. It's built to last. It's extremely thick and full of something called tannin, which insects hate. That's lucky for me, because there's almost nothing worse for a tree than too many bugs. Eat you right up, from the inside out. Also, I'm almost fireproof because of my thick, spongy bark. So I can stand up to most things that threaten other trees.

Q: You said, "*Almost* nothing worse than too many bugs." What's worse?

A: Hate to say it because you are one, but . . . people. In only a fraction of my long lifetime, people have changed things more drastically than all the forces of nature combined. Worse than erosion by wind or climate change. Worse than fire—well, actually many forest fires are caused by people.

Q: But what do people do, specifically?

A: I've seen them cut and burn, burn and cut. Clear the land completely. Settlers moving across the country destroyed millions and millions of acres of woodland starting a few hundred years ago.

Q: Why did they do that?

A: Can't blame them entirely. They needed lumber for shelter, for one thing. One tree my size could make fifty small houses. They took treetops for ship masts. They cleared woods to plant crops. Redwoods were particularly popular because our wood is pretty. It's red at first and weathers to dark red. And our wood is durable. So a lot of redwoods were used for everything from furniture to houses.

Q: So what's wrong with clearing the land?

A: Clear land isn't protected from heat, so it dries out. And there's no root structure to hold it, so it can blow away or erode. By the first part of the twentieth century, 200 million acres of U.S. forests had been cut down. It wasn't long after that 80 million of those acres were unusable even for crops.

Q: But I don't understand. Don't new forests grow back when old ones are cut down?

A: Sure. All it takes is about a hundred years. And a forest doesn't grow right back quite the same. It has to start all over again. Forests go through stages until they're finally back to where they started. Meanwhile the whole ecology of the forest changes.

Q: What do you mean?

A: See, trees perform valuable services to all life. We hold soil in place with our roots, helping to prevent erosion. We draw water up to our leaves or needles and give off moisture, helping to keep things cool. We provide shade so the ground doesn't bake underneath us. We clean the air by taking in carbon dioxide and releasing oxygen.

Q: That's pretty impressive.

A: But it's only one part of the ecology of a forest. Even a small patch of forest can have a thousand different kinds of plants in it. Shrubs, vines, mosses. Herbs and wildflowers. Mushrooms and toadstools. And then there are all the insects, mammals, reptiles, amphibians, and birds that live here. Trees give them food, shade, shelter. We're all connected in here. We're like a sweater someone has knit carefully by hand, full of patterns and color. If one piece of yarn is pulled out, the whole thing can unravel.

Q: So what can be done?

A: Don't destroy forests mindlessly. They have to be managed, with selective cutting and conservation rules and practices followed. Some redwoods are protected now, so we're much safer ourselves. And some other threatened trees have been placed under protection too. But in places like the rain forest, slashing and burning is still going on. We lose 214,000 acres in the rain forest every day, mostly to clear land for crops or cattle. Precious species are being lost, and may take years to come back—if they ever do.

Q: Well, we'll try to spread the word.

A: Please do. I look forward to another thousand years or so.

Activity

ODE TO A TREE Pick a tree that you like. You can look outside or go to a park for inspiration. Why do you like this tree so much? Does the tree attract animals or insects? Why do you think society needs this particular tree? Do you think everyone who passes this tree knows its worth? Write a poem about what this particular tree means to you and Earth. Be sure to include all of the facts that make this tree special and exactly who benefits from the tree's existence.

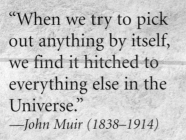

A Tale of Two

Seeing the Light

> "When we try to pick out anything by itself, we find it hitched to everything else in the Universe."
> —*John Muir (1838–1914)*

❖❖❖❖❖❖❖❖❖❖

> "The land is one organism. Its parts, like our own parts, compete with each other and cooperate with each other."
> —*Aldo Leopold (1887–1948)*

These quotes represent the thinking of two of the greatest pioneers in the American conservation movement. John Muir was founder of the Sierra Club and father of the National Parks System. Aldo Leopold was cofounder of The Wilderness Society and father of ecology—the study of the interactions between organisms and their environment. Although the two men grew up a generation apart and led very different lives, they came to share the same basic view: People are part of the natural world, not the center of it.

Muir was born in Scotland and raised on a farm in Wisconsin. John and his younger brother, David, looked forward to rare occasions when they could explore the countryside. "Keep close to nature's heart and break clear away once in a while," he would write in his journal, using ink made from the cones of Sequoia trees. "Climb a mountain or spend a week in the woods. Wash your spirit clean."

Muir had little formal education but read a lot on his own, which helped him in his studies to become an inventor. To avoid being drafted into the Civil War—he said he valued all forms of life too much to kill, even in war—the lanky, bearded young man spent several years hiking through the woods of southern Ontario in Canada. While working at a factory, Muir suffered an injury that left him blind in both eyes. But after several weeks in the hospital he unexpectedly regained his sight. From that moment on, he was determined to enjoy the gift of the great outdoors. Carrying only tea, oatmeal, and bread, he set out on a 1000-mile (1,609-km) journey to the Gulf of Mexico.

Later, in the majestic mountains of California's Yosemite high country, Muir had a spiritual conversion. "Everybody needs beauty as well as bread," he wrote, "places to play and pray in, where nature may heal and give strength to the body and soul." He began to see every rock, plant, and creature as a thread in nature's fabric—a delicate tapestry that could easily be unraveled by man's abuse of the land and its wildlife. In the late 1800s, the United States began paying a high price for its westward expansion. Because of overgrazing by herds of farm animals, reckless hunting by fur trappers, and unregulated tree harvesting by the timber barons, much of our landscape and wildlife were being destroyed.

Muir's passion for nature and for protecting it made him a celebrated champion of the wilderness. His efforts and writings led to the creation of the National Parks System, the U.S. Forest Service, and the preservation of millions of acres of land. More than two hundred natural wonders, including a glacier he discovered in Alaska, are named in his honor. But his greatest legacy is the idea that nature is an integrated whole—that the land and its creatures must be preserved for people to survive on Earth.

Visionaries

Understanding Nature's Gift

Aldo Leopold came to be the John Muir of his generation. He was raised on the bluffs of the Mississippi River near Burlington, Iowa, a place that provided a wonderland of wildlife. Like Muir, as a young boy Leopold had found joy in exploring the wilderness, particularly in hunting. Yet unlike Muir, Leopold was formally trained as a scientist. He earned an advanced degree in forestry and joined the U.S. Forest Service.

While shooting wolves one day, he fired into a pack, later finding a dying mother and her wounded cub. As he watched "the fierce green fire die in her eyes," he said he suddenly discovered "something known only to her and the mountain." From that day forward, his view of hunting changed. He no longer saw it as a sport, but as a disrespectful act to nature. Yet he did not believe that hunting should be controlled. "Game conservation will never succeed merely through repressive laws," he insisted. "It must be founded on a respect for living things."

There were two other experiences that helped shape Leopold's ideas about conservation. In Germany, he witnessed a wilderness so artificially "managed" that it was no longer wild—"deprived of all exuberance." In northern Mexico he saw the opposite—a region where fires burned freely without any permanent damage to the land, and where deer actually thrived among their predators. "I first clearly realized," he wrote after seeing this, "that land is an organism." Leopold began to challenge the custom of controlling forest fires. He argued that this strategy did more harm than good because it altered grazing patterns and increased erosion.

Leopold believed that it was not enough to simply leave the land alone. People had ravaged it, he reasoned, so it was up to people to restore and protect it. But he also understood the challenges of preserving nature in modern society. "All conservation is self-defeating," he said sadly, "for to cherish we must see and fondle, and when we have seen and fondled, there is no wilderness left to cherish. We shall never achieve perfect harmony with land, any more than we shall ever achieve absolute justice or liberty for people. In these higher aspirations, the important thing is not to achieve, but to strive."

Aldo Leopold

Activity

GREAT OUTDOORS Take a trip to your favorite nearby outdoor spot. Make a journal entry of all the natural things you see there and ways in which it could be improved or preserved. What makes this spot special? What would happen to the trees, grass, animals, water, or land if someone decided to build on this spot?

Population Explosion

People Power

The world's human population is about six billion . . . and it's getting bigger every day. Scientists predict that in fifty years it will reach almost nine billion. Many parts of the world are already having trouble dealing with overpopulation and the waste produced by so many people.

Below is a table showing the world's five most populated countries as of 2003, and how scientists predict the top five will read for the year 2050:

Country	2003 Population	Country	2050 Population (Predicted)
China	1,289,000,000	India	1,628,000,000
India	1,069,000,000	China	1,394,000,000
United States	292,000,000	United States	422,000,000
Indonesia	220,000,000	Pakistan	349,000,000
Brazil	176,000,000	Indonesia	316,000,000

Many highly developed European countries expect to see a decrease or slight increase in population. However, the United States' population is expected to increase by 130 million people. And with all these people, there will be much more garbage filling our world.

Respect for Recycling

About 130 million tons of solid waste ends up in landfills each year. Paper is a major ingredient in landfills. It covers 40 percent of landfill space. The average high school student uses 320 pounds (145 kilograms) of paper a year. That sounds like a lot of paper being used, especially when you consider that in 1996, only 42.3 million tons of paper were recycled in the United States—and that's 295 pounds (134 kg) per U.S. citizen.

Newspapers are a big part of the paper problem. If all morning newspapers around the country were recycled, 41,000 trees would be saved each day and 6 million tons (5 million tonnes) of waste would never end up in landfills.

The good news is that Americans are recycling more paper, and it's helping. We now recycle more than 40 percent of all paper used. Now the U.S. paper industry has a new goal for the first few years of 2000: to recycle half of all paper used.

Plastics, including milk containers and some toys, make up about 9 percent of U.S. trash. Plastic soda bottles are actually one of the most commonly recycled products—almost half of those made are currently being recycled.

Things made of metal, including cans, tinfoil, and some appliances, account for only 7 percent of our trash. Aluminum cans are recycled at a rate of 63.2 percent. Thanks to the more than 10,000 recycling centers nationwide, a near record 2 billion pounds (0.9 billion kg) of aluminum were diverted from landfills in 1998 alone.

Approximately 6 percent of our garbage is glass. That's about 87 pounds (39 kg) of glass thrown away by each person each year. Only about 38 percent of glass containers were recycled in 1996. And recycling glass is working. In fact, most bottles and jars now contain at least 25 percent recycled glass.

Waste to Go Little more than one-quarter of our trash, called solid waste, is recycled. This garbage includes everyday items such as product packaging, grass clippings, furniture, clothing, bottles, food, newspapers, appliances, paint, and batteries. What's not recycled is burned or buried in *landfills*—deep-holed plots of land where trash legally can be dumped. Burning releases toxins into the air and creates ash, which needs to be dumped somewhere. The problem with burying trash? The U.S. Environmental Protection Agency says that landfills eventually have to be closed because they fill up or contaminate groundwater. Currently, about 86 percent of U.S. landfills are leaking toxic materials into lakes and streams. Garbage that does not rot, like plastic, can remain in the dirt for *hundreds* of years.

More people on Earth means more businesses will be created to serve them. Businesses such as gas stations, dry cleaners, photo developers, and auto repair shops produce toxic waste products. Hazardous waste—such as gasoline, paint, pesticides, and household cleaners—requires delicate handling. These waste products may have cancer-causing properties, catch fire, or explode easily.

Wastewater, or *sewage*, includes human and animal waste, which increases with the population. All wastewater produced by a city or town passes through a sewage treatment plant. In most wastewater treatment plants, around 90 percent of wastes are disposed of easily because they can break down on their own. But leftover sludge is burned, dumped in the ocean, soil, or a landfill.

Haste Makes Waste

In 1960, each person in the United States was creating, on average, 2.7 pounds (1.2 kg) of garbage each day. Today, with our bigger population and more developed land, each person is producing about 4.6 pounds (2 kg) of garbage every day. Imagine if someone dumped all that garbage in your home each year. Then multiply that by the number of people in your family, and dump that in your house, too. In only a few years, your home would probably be overflowing with this trash.

Now try to imagine a heap of 230 million tons (209 million tonnes) of garbage, which is what the United States produces each year. You could hide a medium-sized city in there. And remember, by 2050 the heap produced each year will be 29 percent bigger!

PHONE BOOKS ONLY NO MAGAZINES CATALOGS

Activity

POPULATION PLUS Find the rate of growth for each country listed in People Power. Use that to determine the year at which China and India could have the same population. Hint: Use the list function on a graphing calculator to find yearly increases.

Wet, Wild, and Worrisome

Water, Water Everywhere!

"Water, water everywhere/Nor any drop to drink." Those words were spoken by a thirsty old sailor in Samuel Taylor Coleridge's poem *The Rime of the Ancient Mariner*. The poor guy was surrounded by water, but it was saltwater, which couldn't quench his thirst. Since we need freshwater to live, the old man's problem is easy to see.

The good news is that Earth's surface is 70 percent water. The bad news is that less than 3 percent of this water is fresh. And only 1/100th of 1 percent of Earth's usable water is available for us to use. More than three-quarters of this freshwater is tucked away, frozen in ice caps and glaciers.

Washington, D.C., 1972

U.S. Congress passes a series of laws called the Clean Water Act, which protects the quality of our nation's water. The mission is to "restore and maintain the chemical, physical, and biological integrity of the nation's waters." The result: Almost every city is required to build a wastewater treatment plant. Plus, states create their own laws to regularly check their water supply for pollution.

Washington, D.C., 1974

Congress passes the Safe Drinking Water Act to protect public drinking water from pollution. It creates laws for cleaning drinking water and offers standards to control waste buildup underground that can pollute water.

Washington, D.C., 1996

In 1996, President Bill Clinton strengthens and changes the Safe Drinking Water Act. The changes ask the states to do more to keep water clean. The president says this is needed because every community is different, and the needs of each water supply may depend on local problems.

Fill 'Er Up!

Most of Earth's water can be found in its oceans. If you decided to drain the world's biggest bodies of water, you could fill more than 100,000 Olympic-sized swimming pools for every single person on the planet!

What Goes Up Must Come Down

Water flows in a continuous cycle that's powered by the Sun. The Sun heats water on Earth's surface, turning it into vapor—that's the "vapor" in the word evaporation. As the vapor rises, it cools and condenses, forming clouds. When the clouds become full with droplets of water, the water comes back down in the form of rain or snow or something in between, such as sleet, hail, or fog.

Water that falls on high ground may move downward in surface runoff. The water collects in rivers, lakes, glaciers, soil, and porous rock, where it is stored temporarily in a process called infiltration. Rivers and streams carry much of this water back into the ocean, where the cycle begins again.

Because the cycle feeds upon itself, changes to one part affect the next. Less rain means less water to evaporate, fewer clouds, very little water in streams, less water to feed plants, and so on.

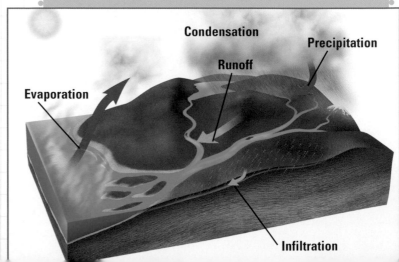

Condensation
Precipitation
Runoff
Evaporation
Infiltration

♪♪♪Singing the Water Blues♪♪♪

High temperatures and no rain create a drought in an already dry part of the country called the Dust Bowl. Hot winds send dried-out dirt flying, ruining farmland and making living difficult for many thousands of people. About 15,000 people die in tragedies related to the drought. Folk singer Woody Guthrie writes "Dust Storm Disaster" about one of the drought's toughest days:

On the fourteenth day of April of nineteen thirty five,
There struck the worst of dust storms that ever filled the sky:
You could see that dust storm coming the cloud looked deathlike black,
And through our mighty nation, it left a dreadful track.

From Oklahoma City to the Arizona line,
Dakota and Nebraska to the lazy Rio Grande,
It fell across our city like a curtain of black rolled down,
We thought it was our judgment, we thought it was our doom . . .

This storm took place at sundown and lasted through the night,
When we looked out this morning we saw a terrible sight:
We saw outside our windows where wheat fields they had grown
Was now a rippling ocean of dust the wind had blown.

It covered up our fences, it covered up our barns,
It covered up our tractors in this wild and windy storm.
We loaded our jalopies and piled our families in,
We rattled down the highway to never come back again.

WATER WORKS

The water we use today has been around since the beginning of time. Imagine dinosaurs drinking our water! Thanks to the never-ending water cycle, this essential resource is continually recycled. But while the amount of water on Earth is unchanging, the amount of clean and usable water is always changing.

Humans and nature together work to maintain a clean supply of freshwater. Flooding can cause pollution by washing waste products into the freshwater supply, just as chemical dumping can. And because the same water is constantly moving from one place to the next, if we contaminate water in one part of the cycle, we risk contaminating it all.

Not a Drop to Drink

Water is not evenly distributed around the globe. The western desert of the United States generally gets little rainfall, while the South gets more than its share. Forty percent of the world's population lives with almost constant water shortages.

Some areas suffer frequent floods; others suffer droughts. In the United States, if an area receives 30 percent or less of its normal rainfall over a period of three weeks or more, we call it a drought.

Activity

THE WATER STORE Most people take for granted the fact that the water that sprays out of our faucets and showerheads is available and clean. Where does your drinking water come from? Research to find a water treatment plant or reservoir—a pool where water is stored—in your neighborhood. How did the water get there? How does it make it into your house?

TIMELINE

DISASTER STRIKES!

Our environment is fragile. Whether caused by human error, greed, carelessness, or weather-related phenomena, accidents have a major impact on the environment. Poisons can reach into the air, soil, and water making major trouble for Earth and its people.

Following are eight of the world's worst environmental accidents. They show that those responsible always have to work hard to fix the damage done—and that even after the cleanup, it may take many years for the people and land to recover.

1948

Where: Donora, Pennsylvania
What: Toxic smog filled with sulfur dioxide and other chemicals.
Who did it: Local factories
How: The smog trapped the toxic air for days.
Who was hurt: 20 people died and 4000 reported trouble breathing.
Consequence: Congress passed Clean Air Act in 1955.

1956

Where: Minimata Bay, Japan
What: Dumping of mercury waste caused "Minimata Disease"—weak muscles and hearing and speaking problems.
Who did it: Chisso Chemical Company
How: People ate the mercury-contaminated fish.
Who was hurt: More than 100 people died, and at least 10,000 others showed symptoms of mercury poisoning.
Cost: $400-500 million
Consequence: Clean up began in 1977 and took 12 years.

1978

Where: Brittany, northwest coast of France
What: 220,000-ton (200-tonnes) oil spill.
Who did it: Amoco Cadiz oil tanker
How: The ship ran aground, and as tug boats tried to free it, the tanker split in two.
Who was hurt: 20,000 birds and millions of marine animals died.
Cost: $85.2 million
Consequence: In the seven months it took to clean the spill, the oil spread to a 230-mile (370-km) area of the Atlantic Ocean. European officials met on the twentieth anniversary of the accident to discuss how to handle and prevent future oil spills.

1984

Where: Bhopal, India
What: Deadly gases from a chemical factory are released.
Who did it: Union Carbide
How: A chemical mixing mistake and poor safety measures.
Who was hurt: 4,000 people died and 300,000 suffered respiratory and neurological illnesses.
Cost: Union Carbide paid $470 million to victims.
Consequence: Two years later, the U.S. Congress passed the Emergency Planning & Community Right-to-Know Act, requiring manufacturers provide a list of the hazardous chemicals they use.

HAZARDOUS WASTE
FEDERAL LAW PROHIBITS IMPROPER DISPOSAL
IF FOUND, CONTACT THE NEAREST POLICE, OR
PUBLIC SAFETY AUTHORITY, OR THE
U.S. ENVIRONMENTAL PROTECT...

1986

Where: Chernobyl, Russia
What: Explosion at the nuclear power plant.
How: Radioactive substances and toxic gases were released into the air.
Who was hurt: 31 people died in the initial explosion, and thousands more were permanently affected by radiation poisoning. Thousands of animals and trees were also killed.
Cost: Estimated health costs are as high as $60 billion.
Consequence: More than 40,000 people were involved in the clean up, which included replacing radioactive soil.

1989

Where: Prince William Sound, Alaska
What: 250,000-barrel oil spill.
Who did it: Exxon Valdez oil tanker
How: The ship hit a rocky reef.
Who was hurt: 1,500 miles (2,414 km) of coastline were damaged; tens of thousands of birds and marine mammals were killed. Oil-drenched animals had to be manually washed to save their lives, a project that cost almost $50,000 for each otter alone.
Cost: Three-year clean up cost $2.1 billion.
Consequence: Officials became more careful about regulating ship traffic in the area. They created a policy requiring each tanker be accompanied by two escort vessels.

1997

Where: Indonesia
What: Out-of-control forest fires destroy one million acres of land, including a rain forest.
Who did it: Companies responsible for clearing land
How: Slash-and-burn clearing—cutting and burning trees rather than paying to remove them—had been a problem for fifteen years. This year, though, a drought turned an environmental crime into a calamity.
Who was hurt: The rain forest is not expected to recover for twenty years.
Cost: $2 billion in lost businesses and health care costs
Consequence: Laws against slash-and-burn clearing had been on the books for two years but hadn't been enforced. Indonesia has strengthened those laws.

1998

Where: Guadiamar River and Doñana National Park, Spain
What: An ore mine's waste-basin wall broke, spilling chemical waste over 25 miles (40 km) of water.
How: The chemicals threatened the park, so workers redirected the contaminated water into the Atlantic Ocean.
Who was hurt: Fish and other marine life were killed; 13,000 acres (5,261 hectare) of land are expected to be unusable for 20 years.
Cost: Farmers estimate that contaminated groundwater cost them $79 million.
Consequence: "Project Doñana 2005" is Spain's plan to keep the park safe from pollution. The government also passed two new laws: a civil responsibility act and an environmental impact evaluation act.

Activity

PROBLEM SOLVER These disasters are large-scale and have led to increased attention to the potential for problems. But there have been many less dramatic environmental problems in the United States alone. What's the best way for you to find out about past problems or potential hazards in your community? Use those resources to find out more about which will affect you the most. What can people in your area do to be sure this problem doesn't get out of hand?

A River Runs Through It

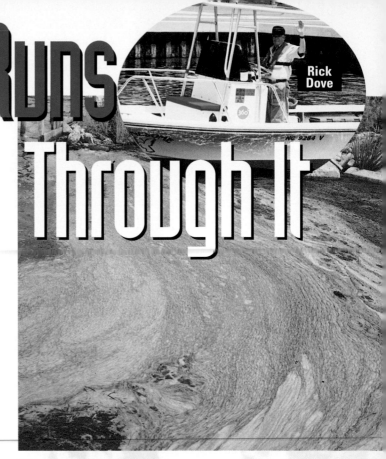

Rick Dove

Waterkeepers are like watchdogs working for Mother Nature. They are dedicated to the preservation and restoration of rivers, bays, and streams.

In 1993, Rick Dove became the first riverkeeper for the Neuse [pronounced noose] River in North Carolina. A retired Marine colonel and attorney, Dove spends his days patrolling the Neuse by boat, plane, and truck, monitoring its condition.

Almost an Ideal Setting

The majestic Neuse River begins near Durham, North Carolina, in the heart of an area of the United States that is attracting more people and businesses than ever. It flows southeast, winding through many cities, farms, and swamps, emptying into Pamlico Sound, a large body of water separated from the Atlantic Ocean by North Carolina's Outer Banks.

Many fish—shad, herring, catfish, bass, flounder —as well as blue crabs and oysters call the Neuse home. And more than 1.5 million people live on its surrounding banks.

But the picture is not as pretty as it could be. The Neuse has been on the top twenty list of threatened rivers in North America. Millions of gallons of partially treated wastewater are dumped into the river each day. Many locations around the river contain high levels of heavy metals like copper, zinc, chromium, and cadmium that can be dangerous to animals and plants. On top of that, hog farming has boomed on the nearby land, where hogs outnumber people by about seven to one. Each day these hogs produce more fecal waste than all the people in the states of New York and California combined.

Disaster Strikes

Rick Dove was already struggling to control the enormous amounts of waste that were affecting the Neuse. As Rick explains, his work became even harder on September 16, 1999: "Hurricane Floyd hit the coast of North Carolina. Thankfully, Floyd had weakened before hitting our area, and by 4 P.M. his winds were a thing of the past. However, his rains would remain for weeks. Hurricane Floyd's 22 inches (56 cm) of rain combined with those of another hurricane to bring a total of 28 inches (71 cm) of rain to parts of eastern North Carolina.

"As the winds slowed down, most people gave a sigh of relief. But they were unaware of the water that would soon endanger not only their homes and property, but their very health as well."

The Things of Nightmares

Dove and his riverkeeper team had to survey the damage by helicopter before fixing it. "As we plotted our course high above the Neuse River on the Friday following Floyd, what we saw in those two and a half hours were the things of nightmares. We saw animal operations whose barns were almost completely covered with floodwater. There were numerous large hog operations where flooding of its lagoons ("pools" where hog waste is stored) released visible plumes of waste into the surrounding waters.

"Finally, we reached the town of Kinston and were even more disheartened by the sites of so many homes and businesses flooded and all the visible pollution. One Kinston wastewater treatment plant was failing, discharging untreated, human waste into the waters of the Neuse. As we continued, we saw numerous junkyards under water. Thousands of flooded cars and commercial businesses were leaching petroleum products into the surrounding waters."

Much of the damage from Floyd was recorded by the North Carolina newspaper, *Raleigh News & Observer*. One article stated that "thousands of hog and poultry carcasses, animal waste from flooded farms, and oil slicks from washed out junkyards and warehouses are polluting (the area), raising concerns about disease and drinking water safety."

Taking Stock of the Damage

Speaking honestly about the environmental impact of Hurricane Floyd, Dove says: "Our immediate concern is the endangerment to human lives from polluted waters. Raw animal waste can contain harmful microbes such as E. coli, which can cause diarrhea, fever, intestinal problems, and occasionally death. Hepatitis A can be contracted from food or water contaminated with human waste, and can cause liver malfunctions, chills, and fever.

"We are also focusing on the short- and long-term effects of this pollution event to our beautiful river. Due to the nutrients and other pollutants discharged into our waters, which can lead to low dissolved oxygen, we need to be watchful for fish kills. At this time we have already encountered measures of low-dissolved oxygen and high levels of pathogens (disease-causing agents).

"Bear in mind that these pollutants will settle to the river bottom, but that does not mean they will remain there. The characteristics of the Neuse, shallow and highly receptive to wind currents, are such that the river bottom is frequently stirred, leading to the resuspension of settled pollutants."

Looking Ahead

"[People think] the river will clean up our mess— act like a waste treatment system. That's nonsense. When bad things get put into the river, they're out of sight and out of mind. This has gotten us into a lot of trouble with our rivers. No one knows for sure how much it will cost to clean up the Neuse, but estimates start at a billion dollars.

"For the longest while, people tried to ignore the Neuse's pollution. Through strong advocacy, our program is bringing about many positive changes in the Neuse. For example, to stop pollution practices we have begun legal actions against a number of polluters, including wastewater treatment plants and hog production facilities.

"The truth is, only the river knows how detrimental pollution will be to us environmentally and economically, and she'll tell us in due time. We can only wonder if we have the resources to cover the debt we now owe to Mother Nature. Let's hope that in her wisdom she allows for all of us to learn from past mistakes."

Polluted water flooded the land because of Hurricane Floyd.

Activity

STORY TIME Choose a river, lake, or ocean located in or near your state, and find five people who can tell you a story related to it. For example, maybe your aunt spent many weekends fishing there because she found plenty of fish. Next, find newspaper articles about that body of water. Do the stories agree with the research? Why or why not? Using the information and stories you found, create your own article about this body of water.

Nature's Own

Each river, tree, mountain, and particle of dirt is unique. It's not just what they contain that makes them special, but also the history that surrounds them.

Protected Parks

One of the first people to suggest a National Parks system was George Catlin, an artist who traveled among Native Americans, sketching them and their pristine homelands. In 1832, Catlin began to worry about the effect westward expansion would have on the Native Americans and the wildlife and wilderness they left untouched. He believed the land should be preserved "by some great protecting policy of government . . . in a magnificent park. . . . A nation's park, containing man and beast, in all the wild and freshness of their nature's beauty!"

Though Congress designated Yellowstone a national park in 1872, it wasn't until August 25, 1916 that President Woodrow Wilson signed an act creating the National Park Service, which was to be responsible for protecting thirty-seven national parks and monuments. Today, the National Park System—which includes national parks, battlefields, historic sites, and seashores, among other sites—focuses on more than 350 areas in North America, providing protected areas for clean water, fresh air, rolling mountains, rich soil, and large forests, among other natural resources.

Established in 1872, the world's first national park, **Yellowstone**, is located mostly in northwest Wyoming but extends into Montana and Idaho. Past volcanic activity is still obvious from the nearly ten thousand hot springs and two hundred geysers, which deposit mineral-rich water that flows back into the soil. Also included in the park are the Grand Canyon of the Yellowstone and many rivers and lakes. Evergreen forests covered 90 percent of the park until fires in 1988 destroyed some of the area.

Located in southeast Tennessee and southwest North Carolina, **Great Smoky Mountains National Park** includes a large hardwood forest (808 sq. miles, 2,093 sq. km). The park has about 600 miles (965 km) of trails, as well as many streams and waterfalls. Many developing businesses in Old Smoky's surrounding states and acid rain have caused some vegetation damage, which the park's officials are trying to reverse.

The western side of the mountains in Washington State's **Olympic National Park** is in one of the areas with the greatest precipitation in the United States; the northeast side is in one of the driest areas on the West Coast. Inside the park's 922,654 acres (373,398 hectares) is Hoh Rain Forest. Sitka spruce and western hemlock are the most common kinds of trees in the rain forest. They can grow as high as 300 feet (91 m). The rain forest also includes mosses, lichens, ferns, and other plants covering every available surface.

River Rights

In his 1997 State of the Union Address, President Bill Clinton created the American Heritage Rivers Initiative. He said he did this "to help communities alongside them revitalize their waterfronts and clean up pollution in the rivers, proving once again that we can grow the economy as we protect the environment."

One of the fourteen protected rivers is New York's **Hudson River**. Considered to be one of America's most important commercial and recreational waterways, the 315-mile- (507-km-) long Hudson travels through nineteen counties where more than eight million people live, work, and play. The Initiative's plan is to help manage the river's water quality and preserve the open space that surrounds it.

There's special dirt in **Capitol Reef National Park**, located in Utah. Cryptobiotic soil—containing soil, cyanobacteria (blue-green algae), lichens, and mosses are important in the area's dry, cold deserts. Unfortunately, because the most important nutrients are on top of the soil, even very little erosion can have a major effect on the soil and the plants that grow in it. When dry, these special soils can be crushed easily by foot or car traffic. But when they are moist, cyanobacteria move through the soil. They leave sticky material on rocks and soil, joining them together, so that the surface becomes more wind and water resistant. This makes the soil great for plant growing.

Activity

SELECTIVE SOIL Find a metal spoon and a dirt patch in your neighborhood. Dig in the dirt a bit until you can make five observations about the soil. Note its colors and what's in it, among other things. What do your observations tell you about the soil? Think about what activities are usually done on or near this soil that may affect its contents. How does what you found relate to the soil's location?

Rollin' Down

It's time to head down South America's Amazon River, the longest river in the world. Humans haven't fully explored the entire river or the surrounding rain forest because some parts are so remote and dangerous. That's why, for this trip, you've turned into a dolphin. Not just any dolphin—a pink dolphin.

There are about 170 of you and your fellow pink dolphins in the Amazon. The river, which is 3,900 miles (6275 km) long, is home to tens of thousands of plant and animal species. This river is so big that it stretches across nine countries in South America, and you can swim through them all! Get your fins ready for a long, tough swim.

You start at your home base—where the Orinoco and Amazon Rivers meet. The water is muddy and brown. This part of the river gets its color from sediment and erosion along the river's banks. As you lift your pointy snout up for a breath of air, you hear a loud, awful sound. BAM!

It's a shotgun. You look into the rain forest surrounding the river just as flocks of birds scatter. Someone in the jungle is shooting. You hear a monkey howl. Hunters in the rain forest kill dozens of animals every day, but it's still a creepy sound.

You duck for cover back into the water and continue your journey up the Amazon. You have to try to steer clear of the discolored, odd tasting parts of the water. Those spots are pollution from waste made by factories and farm chemicals. And because the Amazon contains gold and other elements, mining operations use blasting to get the gold. That means dust and particles—even chunks of rock—are flung into the water. The metal pollution affects the river, as well as the plants and animals in it. Not only are some of the plants your favorite fish eat dying in spots where chemicals have been dumped, but all those chemicals are irritating your skin.

You wonder why people don't see the harm they're causing. Don't they know that many foods and medicines come from the Amazon? You've heard some scientists along the river say that cures for serious illnesses—such as cancer and AIDS—could be found in these plants. They said 121 prescription drugs come from plant sources found in the rain forest. Wow! What an amazing place—and it's your home. But if the plants disappear, not only will you go hungry, but the lifesaving drugs may never be found.

the River

COSTA RICA
PANAMA
Atlantic Ocean
VENEZUELA
GUYANA
SURINAME
FRENCH GUIANA
COLOMBIA
ECUADOR
Amazon R.
BRAZIL
PERU
SOUTH AMERICA
BOLIVIA
Pacific Ocean

All this thinking and swimming is making you hungry. So you head to the bottom of the river to munch on fish. After lunch, you come up for another breath of fresh air. On the riverbanks, you notice people picking fruits and nuts from some of the trees. That's a common sight. More than three thousand fruits are found in the rain forest. Many fruits, vegetables, seeds, and nuts were first discovered in the rain forest. Plus, products like sugar and cacao—the bean used to make chocolate—are found here, too. You start thinking about a big chunk of chocolate, but then you remember you're a dolphin—you eat fish.

Between November and June entire parts of the rain forest flood and become a giant lake. In some areas of the river, the water level rises by as much as 50 feet (15 m). That submerges many areas of the rain forest, which provides food to aquatic animals like you. Knowing this, you can't wait to get to the floodplain. That's where you'll be able to feed on tons of fish that also make an annual journey there.

The floodplain is up ahead. You slow down and look around. The plain isn't as wide as it was last year. It looks like people have cut or burned down many of the trees. There's a large, cloudy area in the water that you find impossible to swim through. When forest is burned, soot and ashes make their way into the river. Not only is it hard to stay clean in this water, but swallowing a mouthful sometimes makes you feel sick. Unfortunately, you know that this is a familiar scene in rain forests around the world. More than 214,000 acres (86,606 hectare) of rain forest are cleared everyday. But you must carry on anyway. You will live here your whole life . . . hopefully the Amazon won't be destroyed much more.

Activity

SAVE THIS PLACE Besides producing 20 percent of the world's oxygen, the Amazon forest offers many resources. Write down three things your government can do to save the rain forests. Keep in mind that we can't pass laws in other countries, but we can encourage them to do things, or at least change the way they interact with the rain forests. Write a letter to your state senator explaining why the rain forest is important and specifically what you think should be done to save it.

Trees Please!

More than 150 years ago, thick forests filled Europe, the Middle East, and parts of the United States. Since 1950, more than 20 percent of these forests have been cut down or intentionally burned. Rain forests—the richest, densest forests near the equator—are currently destroyed at a rate of more than 78 million acres (32 million hectares) a year. Imagine an area the size of Poland filled with trees, and then destroy all the trees. That's the power—and in some places the reality—of *deforestation*.

Deforestation can add up to problems for the environment because trees do an amazing number of things. First, they are part of the water cycle. Through evaporation, their leaves help recycle rainwater into the clouds. Also, their roots help guide soil runoff and infiltration.

The roots of a forest also act as a barrier, helping to keep nourishment for plants and trees in the soil. Removal of trees exposes the rich top layer of the soil, which can cause it to lose nutrients and moisture. Even if rainfall later increases, the soil may be poor for growing.

Deforestation also adds to the climate warming process called the Greenhouse Effect. To clear land, forests are sometimes burned. This is quicker than cutting, and the hope is that some of the leftover ash will provide the soil with nutrients. Yet, in 1987 alone, 10 percent of the heat-trapping carbon dioxide released into the atmosphere was a result of fires intentionally set to clear part of the Amazon rain forest.

Environmentalists attribute forest destruction to its root causes: population growth, economic development, and the need to clear land for farming. The dwindling supply of forests is caused by our increasing need for wood and wood-based products, such as paper. Plus, when the soil is stripped of its nutrients, farmers have to move further into the forests in search of new land. Population growth affects the forests, too, as trees are cleared to make way for cities and roads.

This map shows the world's major concentrations of forests. The graph below compares each area's consumption of both lumber—to make paper and build homes, among other things—and firewood.

Wood Weary

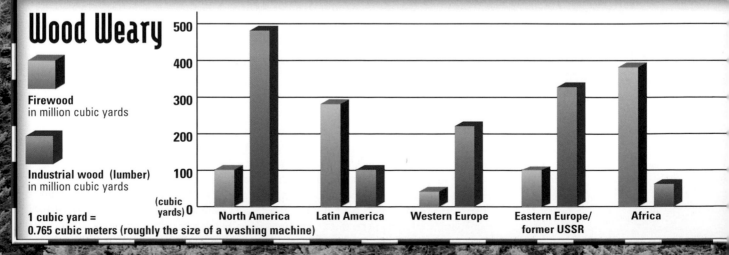

Firewood
in million cubic yards

Industrial wood (lumber)
in million cubic yards

(cubic yards) 0

North America   Latin America   Western Europe   Eastern Europe/ former USSR   Africa

1 cubic yard = 0.765 cubic meters (roughly the size of a washing machine)

Tropical moist forests (evergreen seasonal)

All other forests

Near East

South and Southeast Asia

East Asia

Oceania

Activity

WILD WOOD Developed countries use about 75 percent of the industrial wood, while developing countries use more than 75 percent of the firewood. Why is this true? How can we get both developing and developed countries to use less wood?

Power Producers

Fueling Around

Electrical and chemical energy keep factories churning out products, lights shining, cars running, and the indoors warm, among other things. The fact is those factories use 36 percent of all U.S. energy, while transportation eats up almost 30 percent. And you? People's home, school, and work activities use up another 20 percent.

To produce energy we have to use the resources available to us. Energy can't be created or destroyed. It's the energy source that is used, destroyed, or conserved. Renewable resources are those we can use again and again because they are always being replenished. Nonrenewable resources are those you can use only for a limited time because they are in short supply.

Power from the Past

Fossil fuels give us most of the energy we need to heat our homes, run our cars, and provide electricity. We call them "fossil" fuels because they come from plants and animals that died millions of years ago. Fossil fuels are nonrenewable energy resources such as crude oil (petroleum), coal, and natural gas. Where do we get our fossil fuels? Check out the chart below.

World Watch

- Developed countries use 70 percent of the world's energy.

- The United States has about 5 percent of the world's people, but uses 34 percent of the world's energy.

- The United States imports at least 70 percent of its oil from other countries.

Finding the Fuel

Crude Oil	Coal	Natural Gas
Top five world producers: Saudi Arabia, United States, Russian Federation, Iran, Venezuela	**Top five world producers:** China, United States, India, South Africa, Australia	**Top five world reserves:** Russian Federation, Middle East (Iran, Qatar, United Arab Emirates, Saudi Arabia), United States, Venezuela, Algeria
Top five U.S. producers: Texas, Alaska, California, Louisiana, Oklahoma	**Top five U.S. producers:** Wyoming, Kentucky, West Virginia, Pennsylvania, Illinois	**Top five U.S. reserves:** Alaska, Louisiana, New Mexico, Oklahoma, Texas

Energy Eaters

Some states conserve more than others. While many states are below average in energy consumption, others are above. Why might some states use more than others?

Above Average		High Above Average
Alabama, Arkansas, Delaware, Florida, Georgia, Idaho, Indiana, Iowa, Kansas, Kentucky, Mississippi, Montana, Nebraska,	Nevada, New Mexico, North Dakota, Ohio, Oklahoma, South Carolina, South Dakota, Tennessee, Washington State, West Virginia	Louisiana, Texas, Wyoming

Renewable Resources

The Sun's rays are the basis of solar power. Wind offers a stiff breeze that provides wind power. Water's force when falling creates hydropower. Wherever you find fast moving water, such as in a river or stream, hydroelectricity is possible. Hot water and steam from Earth's crust make geothermal power work. Tides, waves, and water temperature differences are the force behind ocean power. Broken-down matter—such as wood, crops, ocean plants, and food waste—gives biomass energy.

Energy Resource	Advantages	Disadvantages	Did You Know?
Solar power	Inexhaustible, minimal pollution	Sun's rays not consistent, requires large area for collection	*Sunny Days* Numerous solar batteries provide electricity for Coconut Island, off the coast of Australia.
Wind power	Inexhaustible, minimal pollution	Noisy turbines, high winds not found everywhere	*Blowing in the Wind* Besides the United States, other countries increasing their use of wind energy are Germany, Spain, and Denmark.
Hydropower	Little pollution of water or air	Not readily available, dams affect the environment	*Get Wet* Russia houses four of the ten largest hydroelectric plants in the world.
Geothermal power	Inexhaustible, no pollution	Not readily available, must be near source	*Gifted Geysers* Hot springs near Reykjavik, the capital of Iceland, generate nearly enough power for the entire city.
Ocean Power	Lots of coastline to access power	High construction costs, possible negative impact to environment	*Surf's Up!* You'll find tidal power stations in Brittany, France, and Nova Scotia, Canada.
Biomass	Readily available, fuels are efficient and viable	Can contribute to global warming and pollution if burned directly	*Corn on the Car* Ethanol is a fuel made from corn and combines with standard gasoline to conserve fossil fuels.

Nonrenewable Energy Resources

Oil provides us with fuel for transportation, as well as being the basis for other products, such as plastics. Crude oil refers to the raw petroleum substance that is drawn out of the ground. Coal provides electricity when burned. Natural Gas, found in petroleum products, mostly provides us with heat and hot water. Nuclear power splits atoms to create electricity. This is the one unlimited nonrenewable resource.

Energy Resource	Advantages	Disadvantages	Did You Know?
Oil	Available, inexpensive, easy to transport and distribute	Produces carbon dioxide and nitrous oxides, contributes to smog	*Oil Fill* The United States gets most of its oil from Middle Eastern countries.
Coal	Readily available	Causes air and water pollution	*Calling All Coal!* The United States produces 20 percent of the world's coal; almost 280 billion tons (254 billion tonnes) of coal available to mine.
Natural Gas	Clean-burning	Supplies may run out	*Breathe It Out* When we burn natural gas, it produces mostly carbon dioxide and water vapor. When we breathe, we breathe out these same elements.
Nuclear power	Clean, only small amounts needed	Expensive to build plants, dangerous radioactive waste	*Pass the Sunscreen* You would receive more radiation flying round-trip from Los Angeles to New York than if you lived right next door to a nuclear power plant.

Activity

CHART A NEW COURSE Take a look at the chart. Why do you think so few renewable resources are being used? Why might less nuclear energy be used as the years go on? Create a pie chart of what you think the U.S. energy chart for 2050 could look like. Why do you think it will change this way? What can the government do to be sure we use more renewable resources?

We Do Not Inherit the earth from our parents, we borrow it

Earth Day

25th Anniversary

What am I going to do NOW!

Human Error

Earth For All

Former Senator Gaylord Nelson grew up in a small Wisconsin town where every year the area's turtle population would slowly migrate through the woods, over the highway, down Main Street to Mud Lake, where they burrowed into the marsh to survive the winter.

Former Senator Gaylord Nelson was awarded the Presidential Medal of Freedom in 1995.

Nelson and his friends used to carry the turtles safely across the highway. Then, for fun, they'd try to confuse them. "We'd pick them up, spin around six times, put them down behind a tree facing the wrong direction," says Nelson. "They always righted themselves and headed for Mud Lake. I didn't understand how they did it then, and I still don't understand it."

Nelson may not understand the science behind the turtles' trek, but he certainly picked up their determination. For the past five decades, he has stuck to his own path: to make people understand how important the environment is.

Day One

Nelson's dream came a step closer to reality with the first Earth Day, held on April 22, 1970. Not only was that day Nelson's idea, but he's stayed very involved in promoting the worldwide celebrations—speeches, concerts, community cleanup events, and so on—that are held every year on that day ever since. It's an idea that took a lot of time and energy to get off the ground.

Nelson says he became interested in environmentalism simply through enjoying his surroundings. Growing up in the early part of the twentieth century—before television and radio—Nelson spent most of his time outside. He rode horses, skated on frozen ponds, and played with the turtles. Throughout his time in the army, as a lawyer, and as a state legislator, he often read books on nature and wildlife. "At some stage, I became convinced that the most important responsibility in our society is to protect the integrity of Mother Earth's works," Nelson says.

By the time Nelson became Wisconsin's governor in 1958, he had an ambitious plan for conservation in his state. One of the first things he did was to get voters to pass a one-cent tax on cigarettes so that the state could buy one million acres (404,700 hectares) of land for a wilderness preserve.

Ecological problems weren't limited to Wisconsin, though, and Nelson wanted the world to know about the problems facing the environment. "Government doesn't do anything if it's not on the agenda, and the environment just wasn't," says Nelson.

Building a Plan

Nelson's first idea for how to get his colleagues in politics to pay attention to the environment was a flop. While he was still governor and running for the U.S. Senate, he asked President Kennedy to make a five-day tour of eleven states to discuss conservation.

In September 1963, Kennedy, Nelson, and two other senators began the tour. "When we got on the plane, we were with 75 or 80 members of the media, and I remember thinking, 'Well, this is it. This will put the issue on the national agenda.'" Unfortunately, he was wrong. The press only wanted to talk to the president about what they saw as a more immediate concern: a treaty against nuclear testing that the Senate had approved that day.

Nelson didn't give up hope. He decided that going straight to the people was the way to get the issue the most attention. Between 1963 and 1969, he visited thirty-five states that were having environmental problems and found large audiences in each one. "As is often the case, the public was way ahead of the politicians," Nelson says.

Time for Action

By 1969, the United States was starting to have environmental crises too big to ignore. Many beaches had to be closed because of pollution. Problems such as acid rain and smog were becoming commonplace. The Cuyahoga River in Ohio was so contaminated with chemicals it actually caught fire.

Nelson had just visited Santa Barbara, California, where there had been a disastrous oil spill, when he read an article on the anti-Vietnam War teach-ins that were happening across the country. Students at colleges and universities had been gathering to speak about a peaceful solution to end the war. The idea inspired him to do the same for the environment.

The next day, he announced his plan for a nationally celebrated day to think about the environment. Hundreds of phone calls poured into his Washington, D.C., office from people who wanted to participate in the first celebration before the senator had even picked a date. He finally chose April 22, so that kids in college wouldn't be on spring break or in exams.

The first Earth Day was a huge success with an estimated 20 million people participating around the country. "My goal was to have a demonstration so large it would shake up the establishment and force this issue permanently onto the national political agenda," Nelson says. "It was a gamble, but it worked."

Easy as One, Two, Tree!

It doesn't have to take years to get a plan to help get the environment rolling. Patricia Arambula, 15, and Iris Ybarra, 16, students at South San Antonio High School in San Antonio, Texas, began a program to plant trees at their school to help fight air pollution.

It all began when a science club advisor taught them how helpful trees were. He told them that trees absorb carbon dioxide—the main gas that causes the "greenhouse effect," which is responsible for global warming. Plus, trees planted next to a building can block the Sun's direct rays, allowing less energy to be used indoors for air conditioning.

Amazed by this information, the girls organized a tree planting club at school. After researching which trees would grow best in their area, they raised money to buy trees through garage sales, donations from the community, and a schoolwide recycling program. Working after school and on weekends, the club planted almost 100 trees and shrubs. The project is now a permanent science club activity at their school.

Activity

PLAN AHEAD Choose an environmental problem and develop a way to let the world know how important it is. If you could hold one event or create one material to get global attention, what would it be? Write an outline for your proposal, including why everyone should care about the problem, who you'll need to get involved in the project (organizations or celebrities), and how you think your proposal will make a positive change for the world.

Dirty Deed

There are only two ways to get to the movies: Have your parents drive you or walk on a shortcut that takes you through the woods.

"Where are you off to?" your mom calls out, as you and three friends gather on the side of the street.

"Movies," you mumble. She should know by now that you go every weekend.

"Want a ride, or are you walking again?"

"Uh, walking, but thanks."

"Okay, just be careful. And watch out for the Crabapples. You know they don't like you crossing their garden."

The Crabapples—Mr. and Mrs., that is. There's no way you can forget them. The shortcut over the muddy stream and through the forest to the movie theater takes twenty minutes.

You—and everyone else in your neighborhood—go so often that you've worn a little footpath. The worn trail actually makes you feel safer walking through the woods. The problem is that this path cuts right through the Crabapples' tomato garden.

Every year, their tomato plants win top prize at the state fair, but that doesn't make the Crabapples any happier. They hate to see people in their garden. You and your friends feel like you have no choice but to pass through it.

Today, as you and your friends pass the Crabapples' backyard, you are stopped in your tracks.

"Just hold on a minute!" says Mr. Crabapple, camera in hand. His bald head is wrinkled with anger as his eyes widen. "Didn't I tell you kids to get off my land? You don't listen and now I've caught you in the act—on film. I'm taking this to the town council. They'll have you arrested. You kids, you've ruined my tomato garden. Last year there were fewer than usual, but they didn't come up at all this year. First time in 25 years—25 years I've been planting here—that my garden won't be represented at the fair. I work hard out there. Every other day I weed and turn over the loose dirt. I even ripped all the trees that were around it out . . . to give my plants more space to grow. Now there are no plants, no tomatoes. It's all your fault. I'll sue your parents!"

marched up their back steps and into the house.

The next morning your mom wakes you up early.

"A member of the town council just called," she said, looking very worried. "They want us all to come for a meeting tonight. It seems that the Crabapples can't grow anything in their garden anymore. The dirt's just dry and ruined. The council member said she wants to have the Crabapples speak, then you and your friends can say what you need to. Then, the council members will have to decide what to do. You father thinks they can fine us!"

"Don't worry, Mom. I'll take care of it," you say, yawning. But you feel awful. Could it have been all your fault? How will you take care of this mess? Immediately you think of Brittany. She's your smartest friend in town; she can be the one to do all the talking.

A quick phone call to Brittany reminds you of only one problem. She didn't go to the movies with you yesterday and so she's not in the picture the Crabapples have. That must be why the councilmember never called her family. You tell her what happened at the Crabapples' yesterday.

"I'll help you out," says Brittany. "But I'm leaving for my grandmother's in half an hour. If I write you some notes, they'll make it easier for you to argue that it's not all your . . . I mean, our, fault. If we suggest ways to help the plants grow in the future, they may like that, too. Come by and pick up the notes."

After getting dressed, you run over, only to find Brittany gone. She did leave you some notes, though. Now it's your job to figure out why the Crabapples' garden may have stopped growing.

"You kids have been walking over this land for too long—twenty-something years!" says an angry Mrs. Crabapple.

You speak up: "Excuse me, Mr. Crabapple, Mrs. Crabapple, but I don't think you can say this is all our fault."

"Who cares what you say now," interrupts Mrs. Crabapple. "You can speak in front of the law. We have no time for this. Come on, Henry." With that, the Crabapples

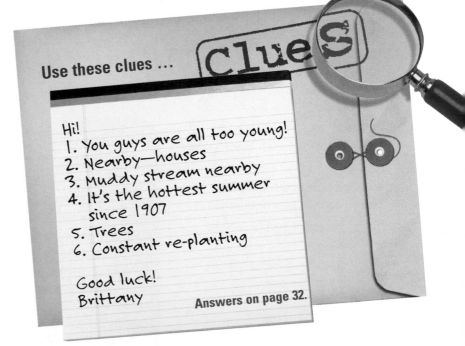

Use these clues ... clues

Hi!
1. You guys are all too young!
2. Nearby—houses
3. Muddy stream nearby
4. It's the hottest summer since 1907
5. Trees
6. Constant re-planting

Good luck!
Brittany

Answers on page 32.

Earth Day

Traveling Trash

Some states get rid of their trash by selling it to others. One example of this came in the form of a "garbage barge," a boat full of 3,186 tons (2,891 tonnes) of trash that left Islip on Long Island, New York, in early 1987. It traveled for six months, trying to dock in ports in North Carolina, Louisiana, Florida, Mexico, Belize, and the Bahamas. When no one else would accept it, the floating trash heap ended up traveling back to Long Island.

Wrong Way Renewables

Back in 1837, a 24-foot- (7-m-) high dam was built on Maine's Kennebec River. Stretching 917 feet (280 m) across, it was built to supply hydroelectric power to factories along the river's banks. But in the process, it blocked salmon, shad, and herring, among other fish, from swimming upstream where they had been mating for over a century. In 1997, the federal government decided the dam had to be torn down to restore the environment. Although the owners weren't happy, the dam came down in October 1999. Only a month later, fishermen said they noticed more fish in the river.

Workers take apart Edwards Dam on the Kennebec River.

Save Your Energy

CAN YOU GUESS WHICH APPLIANCE USES THE MOST ENERGY?

1. Desk fan, iron, incandescent light bulb, or 16-inch black and white TV set

2. Average computer, blender, ceiling fan, or air conditioner

3. Hair dryer, microwave, stove, or stereo

4. Vacuum, 26-inch color TV set, VCR, or toaster oven

Answers on page 32

Slicker Than Oil

Almost 14,000 oil spills are reported each year in the United States alone. Many are small, but what's the best way to clean up the big ones? One controversial idea suggests having bacteria, molds, and yeast eat the oil. They are able to digest it and turn it into less harmful waste.

Oil is naturally made, but organisms that can gobble it up have to be made in laboratories. And scientists are unsure if it's best to encourage the growth of these bacteria in areas prone to oil spilling. After all, what if these "helpers" cause more problems for the land and water? Unfortunately, their full impact on the environment is unclear since this idea is so revolutionary.

Plant Life

When life first began on Earth more than 2 billion years ago, the only plant life was in the sea. Our land was bare until about 425 million years ago. That's when moss—that you may now find in shady, dark places—began growing. By the time dinosaurs walked Earth, there were more complicated plants, including tall ferns. Pines, redwoods, and other cone-bearing trees developed later—about 3 million years ago.

SYMBOLS MADE SIMPLE

Have you ever seen those numbers inside a recycling symbol on a plastic container? To help recyclers sort materials, the Society of the Plastics Industry has developed a coding system for plastic containers. Each code number refers to what material is used to make the product.

Example	Code
Soft drink bottles	1
Milk and water containers	2
Shampoo bottles	3
Ketchup bottles	4
Squeeze bottles	5
Fast food packaging	6

WOOD WISE

- One of the world's toughest trees is Argentina's ombu tree. Its wood is so moist that it will not burn and so spongy that it can't be cut.
- Almost half of tree wood goes to build homes; another 30 percent is used for making paper.
- One medium-sized tree can only make enough paper for about 400 newspapers.
- In the United States, an average of 267 pounds (121 kg) of newspaper is now recycled from each person each year.

Green Garbage

Landfills in Wisconsin, Florida, Minnesota, and Illinois, among other states, have put a ban on accepting leaves, grass clippings, and other yard wastes from businesses and homeowners. These natural items make up about 20 percent of the garbage in many landfills.

Food Fills the Forest

These originated in rain forests: tomatoes, cinnamon, black pepper, oranges, bananas, and paprika.

Anti-Acid

Waste gases from cars and factories rise into the air. These gases then mix with water vapor in the clouds to form acids. The polluted rain that falls from these clouds is called *acid rain*.

- By attacking plant leaves and the soil, acid rain weakens trees which fall sick and eventually die. Over half the trees in West Germany's huge Black Forest have been damaged by acid rain.

- Acid rain is a problem for the 6 million acre (2 million hectare) Adirondack State Park. Of the small percentage of lakes that have been tested for acid rain pollution there, 170 show damage from acid rain. As a result, they have no fish living in them.

31

This Land is Your Land

Written in 1787, the U.S. Constitution serves as a guide for the who, how, and why of running the government. The people who wrote the Constitution are all long gone, but the United States needs another constitution—an environmental one.

The president is busy with foreign affairs, and Congress and the Supreme Court have an unusually heavy load of work, but they all agree that conserving our environment is a major concern. So much so, in fact, that they have decided to hire some young men and women who know a great deal about natural resources and the problems we face in conserving them to design this second constitution. That's where you come in.

Create a constitution based upon the principles of how to live without hurting the environment. Make sure you include an opening statement about why the document is necessary. You may gain inspiration for this section by researching Native American thoughts and proverbs about the environment. Then, cover the principles the nation should follow in protecting its natural resources. Looking at a copy of the 1787 Constitution may be helpful. In fact, your constitution should uphold the rights of the U.S. Constitution. You can't make an environmental constitution that's illegal! You also need to also keep in mind that there will be plenty of opposition to any idea that may hurt businesses or the economy.

Answers
Solve-It-Yourself Mystery, page 28:

Standing up in front of the city council is tough, but you do it anyway. If you mention all of these things, you have no fine to pay: First of all, it's not just your fault because the whole neighborhood has been walking that path for more than twenty years, as the Crabapples pointed out. Plus, if they have been planting in the same place for more than twenty years, the nutrients and moisture in the soil may be weak. And their constant gardening may have loosened soil. The fact that they have no trees doesn't help plant growth either, since the trees could offer nutrients and help with soil infiltration—so that rainwater can easily get to the crops. Without trees, the soil is completely exposed—it can easily lose moisture and nutrients in its rich top layers. Furthermore, it's summer, which means it's dry and the soil can easily be blown away. The muddy stream nearby would explain where all the loose soil has gone.

Tell the Crabapples to plant trees around the garden and add more nutrients to the soil or move the garden if they want things to grow in the future.

Fun & Fantastic, Save Your Energy, page 30:
1. Iron
2. Air conditioner
3. Stove
4. Vacuum